Things To Do in Young People's Worship

Susan Sayers

Kevin Mayhew

First published in 1997 by
KEVIN MAYHEW LTD
Rattlesden
Bury St Edmunds
Suffolk IP30 0SZ

© 1997 Kevin Mayhew Ltd

Adapted from *Including Young People* (Kevin Mayhew, 1996)

0 1 2 3 4 5 6 7 8 9

ISBN 1 84003 017 8
Catalogue No 1500121

Front cover: *Sunlit Crowd* by Diana Ong.
Courtesy of SuperStock Ltd, 72/74 Brewer Street, London

Cover design by Jaquetta Sergeant
Typesetting by Louise Hill
Printed in Great Britain

Foreword

While many churches provide for the needs of children, there is often an uncomfortable gap where young people are concerned. This is the age when deep questions are being asked, and it is essential that our young people find in their churches those who are going to listen and not be shocked; who are willing to enter into real discussion and provide relevant and unsuffocating support during adolescence.

Many churches are well aware of the needs, but find it difficult to provide for them. They are concerned about this age group feeling too old for children's ministry but not able to relate to what the adults are doing in church. Sadly, the result is often an exodus of young people, just when their faith could be (and often is) taking off.

Not only do our young people need the church; the church badly needs its young people. Their insistence on rejecting every hint of hypocrisy and their gift of presenting challenging ideas with wit and enthusiasm – these are good for everyone and vital for a healthy body of Christ.

This book aims to provide relevant and varied activities for young people, which stimulate their thinking and encourage valuable discussion. Although some young people will be involved in the children's ministry team, I am convinced that they need to be provided for at their own level as well. Sometimes I have suggested that the young people put their ideas to the wider church. Do encourage the church to take such ideas seriously.

A note about role-play

Improvising a drama is a very effective way of helping people get 'under the skin' of Bible and other stories. Precisely because of that, it is vitally important for the leader to 'de-role' the actors after it. This is simply and effectively done if the leader goes round the group asking each one to say his or her name, where they are and to define their real relationship with other actors, e.g:

What's your name?
  Joanna Harrison.

Where are you?
  Bethany Baptist Church youth group.

And do you *really* hate Karen?

No, that was just an act. We're friends.

This can be done in a very light-hearted way, adding to the fun of the role-play itself, and may seem quite trivial. However, for people of any age who have 'thought themselves into' a part, it's absolutely essential they 'talk themselves out of it'.

I hope the ideas in this book will enable young people in the churches to grow strong and healthy in their faith.

SUSAN SAYERS

Contents

GOD OUR CREATOR
AND REDEEMER

This is God's earth

Thought for the day   This earth is God's earth.

Things to read   Psalm 104
Job 38:1-21; 42:1-6
Acts 14:8-17

Things to do   *Aim:* To help them understand that God can work through us with power.

Read the story in Acts together, with people taking active parts if they enjoy that sort of thing. Otherwise, have different people reading, two at a time if there are any with reading difficulties. How could ordinary people like Paul and Barnabas heal this lame man? Draw their attention to the way the healing happened, and the words that were said. It was still Jesus doing the healing, just as he had when he was there among people in Galilee.

Now for the daft bit . . . have two model cars – one a really smart, powerful car, the other with a far less powerful engine. Get everyone to make the right type of engine noises for each one as you push them along on the flat. The real difference becomes apparent when you're accelerating out of a roundabout up a hill. Make a clipboard into a hill and try the small car first. Now try with the powerful model and see (and hear!) the difference.

To work powerfully for God in this world we need the power of God right inside our lives. With God living in us we shall all be 'powerful models'. The more empowered Christians there are in this area, the more powerful will be the effects for good, and for healing.

Things to discuss   1 Do you ever find God's power frightening? Should it ever be frightening?

2 The Acts reading raises the question of God answering our prayers for healing. Sometimes he doesn't appear to. What factors may be involved here? Should we be going about things differently?

God rescues and redeems us

Thought for the day

God is a rescuer and redeemer of his people.

Things to read

Psalm 66
Exodus 1:8-14, 22-2:10
Hebrews 3

Things to do

Aim: To familiarise them with the background to the Moses rescue.

Have a collection of library books providing information on the Israelites in Egypt and ask the group to find out what they can about:

1 how the Israelites came to be in Egypt

2 how they were now being treated by the Egyptians and why.

They can do this in twos and threes.
   Come together and discuss the findings, noting the main points on a flip chart. In the light of this discussion, read the Exodus passage together. Think together about:

1 why Moses' mother put her son in a basket

2 why it would help for the Israelites' rescuer to have been familiar with the Egyptian way of life

3 how God was responding to the Israelites' cry for help.

Things to discuss

1 To what extent do we sometimes actively prevent God from rescuing or healing in some situations?

2 Bearing in mind the Moses story, sort out the difference/ similarity between total trust in God and personal effort.

Real life + real death = real redemption

Thought for the day

Jesus could only buy us full life by submitting to full death.

Things to read

Psalm 66
Isaiah 53:7-end
Matthew 27:33-54

Things to do

Aim: To understand the link between the crucifixion and the Isaiah passage of the suffering servant.

Read the passage from Isaiah first, asking them to think about who it reminds them of. Then read the gospel passage, involving as many readers as possible, and follow it with a worship chorus such as *Such love, pure as the whitest snow* or *You laid aside your majesty*.

Try to put yourselves into that time before the resurrection and think about whether you might have got angry at Jesus not saving himself, and doubted his claim to be the Son of God. You could use the role-play technique here, with a group of onlookers under the cross talking about the man who hangs dying above their heads. De-role the players (see Foreword) and end with a time of quietness and prayer.

Things to discuss

1 What can we learn about the crucifixion that will help us when faced with the problem of suffering?

2 People often say, 'If only . . . then I'd believe.' What is misguided about this way of thinking?

The triune God

Thought for the day

God is creator, redeemer and life-giver all at once, in every situation.

Things to read

Psalms 29, 33
Exodus 34:1-10
Acts 2:22-36

Things to do

Aim: To explore how the Trinity came to be expressed as such.

Begin by having a juggling session, using light scarves, juggling balls or rolled-up socks or anything else 'jugglable'. Make sure there are enough for everyone to have a go, and see if anyone can manage to keep three balls going at once. Enjoy their performance.

Have the doxology written up so everyone can see it. They may have come across this during worship; say it together now. Look into the meaning to discover how many persons are being worshipped in this prayer. Encourage discussion about what the Trinity explains, and point out that in a way this is like trying to juggle with ideas about God. We are attempting to hold all our knowledge of God at once, so as to keep as close to the truth as possible.

Look at Peter's sermon after the coming of the Holy Spirit, to see how the idea is expressed of God being three persons yet one God.

Work out together what you believe about God the Father, God the Son and God the Holy Spirit, and form this into a chant, rap or set of responses that could be used in worship as a statement of faith.

Things to discuss

1 The Exodus reading makes it clear that Moses had a remarkable understanding of God. What can we learn from Moses' life which might give us some advice for ways in which we could grow closer to the God we worship?

2 Think of church architecture through the centuries and see how this has expressed in solid form the aspects of God which have been emphasised at different times. What are the dangers of highlighting aspects of God?

In Christ we can all belong

Thought for the day   In Christ we can all belong – he has broken the barriers down.

Things to read   Psalms 85, 133
Ezekiel 37:15-end
Ephesians 2:11-end

Things to do   *Aim:* To help them understand the reasons for splits in God's people, both now and then.

Beforehand, search out some clear maps of Old Testament events. I have found these particularly helpful:

> *The Atlas of the Bible* – Readers' Digest
> *Atlas of Bible History* – Lion
> *The New Bible Atlas* – Lion

Begin by having a short, anecdotal discussion of times when they and you have been in the kind of awful situation that doesn't seem to have any hope of a solution.

Using the maps and information books, explain how the kingdom came to be split, and take the story as far as the exile. At this point read together the passage from Ezekiel, so that they will be better able to appreciate how the people would have felt as they heard this prophecy. Follow this with the New Testament reading to see how the prophecy came true.

What about now? Collect a list of all the different Christian denominations they can think of, and talk together about the sadness of disunity in the Church and the need for unity rather than uniformity. Make a note of ideas which come out of the discussion as you think prayerfully about what we can do to draw Christians together, and look at what is already happening. If it seems appropriate, plan the outline of an interdenominational activity and worship which could be used in the not too distant future.

Things to discuss   1 Look at a chart of events in the Old Testament to see what had happened to the people of Israel to make them two separate states, and where they were when this prophecy was written.

2 How can your church ensure that visitors sense the truth of Ephesians 2?

The cost of our redemption

Thought for the day

Christ had to suffer in order to rescue us.

Things to read

Psalm 119:105-120
Exodus 5:1-6
Luke 22:54-end

Things to do

Aim: To help them understand the implications of the readings in our own lives.

Read the passage from Exodus with different people taking various parts and everyone reading the parts spoken by the people of Israel. Have a Venn diagram drawn on a chart like this:

and a selection of words to describe their feelings. They can discuss where to place the words, and they can add other ideas of their own. Here are some suggestions to start you off: angry, bitter, resentful, defensive, cunning, greedy, disillusioned, confused, doubting, isolated, embarrassed, ridiculed.

Now read the gospel passage and try another Venn diagram, this time looking at Jesus, Peter and Judas.

Remind them of how Moses went on to lead his people to freedom, and Jesus went on to save us from the slavery of our sin and give us full life. Help them to see how the dark patches in our lives may well be the way forward to something far better than we could dream of. Pray together for trust and courage in the dark times.

Things to discuss

1 If a prayerfully planned innovation at church or in the locality starts meeting violent opposition, can we assume that it is against God's will, or could there be other factors at work?

2 What do you think was in the look that Jesus gave Peter when the cock crowed?

Our great and timeless God

Thought for the day   The earth is the Lord's.

Things to read   Psalm 104
Proverbs 8:1, 22-31
Revelation 21:1-7, 22-end

Things to do   *Aim:* To consider the vast and timeless nature of God.

Read both readings with the group, being sensitive to poor or embarrassed readers by having people read in twos or threes if necessary. After the Proverbs passage, guide them into seeing the link between Wisdom and the character of Jesus. Draw their attention to the words in Revelation: 'I am the beginning and the end'.

How can God not have a beginning? Surely everything starts somewhere? Allow doubts to surface and discuss them, respecting all opinions. In order to mature in faith, it is essential that young people feel able to talk through their doubts without feeling criticised.

Have the word GOD written up on a large sheet of paper. Show how the very centre of God is like a circle – without beginning or end. After singing a quiet worship chorus, sit together in complete stillness for a while to become aware of the present moment. Enjoy the peace of God which becomes noticeable in our stillness. While everyone is still relaxed and peaceful, tell them quietly how God living for ever doesn't mean that he's really old – it means that he always *is*, as we can feel him now. Whether we were living five hundred years ago, or now, or in the next century, that wouldn't change. God loves us, and in every age, he is.

Things to discuss   1 The Trinity is not mentioned by name in the Bible. Discover how it is described implicitly in these readings.

2 If we really believe that the earth belongs to our God so completely, why do we need to work at looking after it?

God is our hope and its fulfilment

Thought for the day

In his own good time, God is drawing all things to perfect completion.

Things to read

Psalms 23, 24 or 78:1-24
Ezekiel 34:11-24
2 Peter 3

Things to do

Aim: For them to explore the nature of the hope to which we are called.

First read the passage from Ezekiel, picking up any ideas here that they recognise from the New Testament. Join these together, so that they can see how Jesus' ministry brought to fulfilment the hopes and longing of the people of Israel.

Now read the letter from Peter and explain the climate of feeling at the time he was writing. Talk together about how they feel, knowing that Jesus could return at any time. Are there any areas in our lives which we need to sort out with God before we can look forward to it? We need to clear up anything outstanding every day, as we never know when it might happen. Have a time of quietness and worship, per- haps jotting down anything they want to put right with God on a piece of paper which is then put in a sealed envelope and only thrown away when completed.

Things to discuss

1 Go through the Ezekiel passage, linking up each section with its remarkable fulfilment in the life and teaching of Jesus.

2 We are now about two thousand years on from the time of Jesus, and the Church has had a stormy and sometimes shameful journey through time to the present. What do you think we have learnt from this, and what should we be concentrating on in the next few years, do you think?

Safe in the hands of God

Thought for the day

Whatever may happen to us, ultimately we shall be safe in the hands of the living God.

Things to read

Psalms 30, 48
Deuteronomy 4:25-40
Revelation 2:1-11

Things to do

Aim: To recognise God's love which challenges and keeps us safe.

Read the Deuteronomy passage together and look at a biblical atlas to see where the people of Israel had come from, reminding one another of what happened where. All these events gave them a powerful experience of God so that they knew they could rely on him.

Have a browse through some literature about ways to serve God in challenging situations, such as VSO, Action Aid, Christians Aware, Feet First, Operation Gideon and Time for God, just to get them thinking for the future. If there is anyone in the community who has recently been involved with such a venture, invite them in to join the discussion so that questions and doubts can be raised and talked through.

Pray together for God to govern our lives in the future, wherever that may lead. Exciting, isn't it!

Things to discuss

1 Since we all find it impossible to walk without sin all the time, how can we ensure that we don't stray too far, and how can we find our way back?

2 For what might the churches today be praised and criticised? What in them do you think pleases God and what saddens him?

GOD WITH US

God becomes vulnerable

Thought for the day   Laying his glory and majesty aside, God is content to enter human life as a vulnerable baby.

Things to read   Psalm 132
Haggai 2:1-9
1 Peter 2:1-10
Luke 2:41-end

Things to do   *Aim:* To help them understand God's loving restoration programme.

You will need a selection of things which need restoring in some way, and the equipment for putting them right, e.g:

tarnished silver
socks which need darning
guide/scout blackened pots and pans
a badly wired plug.

First read the passage from Haggai and talk about the way God gets involved with people who are in ruins and lovingly restores them. It was for this reason that Jesus was born into our world.

Now set everyone restoring the things you have brought, and talk as you all work about the different ways that sin ruins people's lives and how there is always hope because Jesus lives in and amongst us. When we offer to build with him we may be used in quite unexpected ways.

Things to discuss   1   Having read all these passages, what practical help can we find about the most effective restoration work whenever it is needed in our own lives, in our church community and in society?

2   In the light of the Haggai reading, what significance is there in the Luke story for this week?

God's amazing humility

Thought for the day

Christ's amazing humility is to be our perfect example.

Things to read

Psalms 108, 110
Jeremiah 31:1-13
Philippians 2:1-8

Things to do

Aim: To help them understand that Jesus is in glory and his kingdom is spreading.

First read the Jeremiah passage and talk about how it can sometimes be good for us to have to put up with hardship and discomfort from time to time. Make a list of what good can come out of such situations.

Now look at the Philippians passage. Have some world maps which are marked to show how Christianity has spread outwards from Jerusalem. Talk about how God's kingdom is still spreading, and if possible show some pictures of worship in areas where Christianity is growing fast at the moment. What aspects of our society have been changed for good through the influence of Christians? What prevents more being done?

Pray for all people who are deeply involved with peace-making, justice, aid and so on, and write letters or postcards of encouragement to some of them.

Things to discuss

1 Do we dare to put aside all the credibility, popularity or status we crave in order to follow Christ in such a total, self-emptying way? Do we even want to?

2 Look at each area of your life and tackle any weeds of self-deception, self-seeking or ambition you find. In God's presence, with your eyes fixed on Christ, lay them aside and ask God to fill the emptied areas with love.

A ministry of healing and prayer

Thought for the day God knows us inside out.

Things to read Psalm 139:1-8
2 Kings 4:8-37
Mark 1:21-end

Things to do *Aim:* To look at Jesus' healing/prayer ministry.

First go through the gospel reading with these questions written on a chart:

Who?
Where?
When?
How?
So?

and fill the chart in as you find the information.
   Notice how Jesus undergirds all his ministry with long times of prayer. Discuss your own prayer commitments in the light of Jesus' example, being practical and encouraging.

Things to discuss 1 Make a note of everything the Shunamite woman does and everything Elisha does. What can we learn from this about faith?

2 What do you notice about Jesus' prayer/work balance? Check your own input/output against this model.

Jesus really died that we might really live

Thought for the day Jesus could only buy us full life by submitting to full death.

Things to read

Psalm 66
Lamentations 3:19-33
Luke 23:26-49

Things to do

Aim: To look at the crucifixion through the eyes of those present.

First read the account of the crucifixion in Luke, with people reading the different parts.
   Have a chart divided into three columns.
   Make a list together of the people mentioned. Put them in one column and beside each name jot down how they behaved towards Jesus and what may have been the underlying reason for their behaviour. This close study will help build a realistic picture of the events, and will highlight the attitudes and behaviour in our own faith journey which can be acknowledged and better understood.

Things to discuss

1 What does Jesus' attitude to suffering have to help us as we struggle to make sense of apparently pointless suffering in our own lives?

2 Look at the different attitudes of the criminals crucified with Jesus, and at Jesus' response to them.

Christ reveals the glory of God

Thought for the day   God empties himself to glorify humanity.

Things to read   Psalm 132
Isaiah 40:18-end
Colossians 1:1-20

Things to do   *Aim:* To help them appreciate the glory of God and his generous love.

Begin with a time of praise and worship, reading the Isaiah passage together with taped/live music playing in the background. Then ask the group to plan some way of expressing the wonder of God which this passage describes. They can use art work, three-dimensional structure, music, dance or mime for instance, or a mixture of media. This can be incorporated into the worship either today or next week.

Things to discuss   1 What difference would it make to our world if more people realised the extent of God's power?

2 What does this way of saving people tell us about the character of God?

The grace of God

Thought for the day God gives us the grace necessary to reveal his glory.

Things to read Psalms 46, 47
Isaiah 61
Ephesians 2:1-10

Things to do *Aim:* To explore the way God's grace enables us to show God's glory.

First talk about allergies, sharing the gory details of any they or their friends have when they eat or touch something they are allergic to. Point out that the people concerned don't work at making that rash or asthma attack – it happens naturally, as a result of contact with a particular substance.

Now think about good automatic reactions, such as feeling less hungry through eating, less tired through sleeping, being able to get through a locked door if you use a key, or smelling good through dabbing on perfume or aftershave. Again, these things happen quite naturally as long as the right input is given.

Read the beginning of the Isaiah passage together. What happens as a result of the Spirit of the Lord being upon him? (Jesus used this passage to refer to himself.) There is both a commissioning and an enabling.

Read the Ephesians passage, and see how God's grace enables us to work God's love in a natural way – we won't have to contort ourselves out of shape because God will work within us the way we are, using our gifts and talents, but also our weaknesses, whereas if we fight against accepting and using his grace, we make life unnecessarily hard for ourselves.

Things to discuss 1 How do we sometimes prevent God from providing the grace we need, rather than want, in our lives?

2 Work through the Isaiah reading, noting the practical ways in which Jesus displayed God's grace and glory in his ministry.

God's presence changes things

Thought for the day

After years of waiting, the Lord is very near.

Things to read

Psalm 40
1 Samuel 1:1-20
Luke 1:39-55

Things to do

Aim: To think about doing things God's way.

First read the story of Hannah, with different people taking parts or acting it out. Look at why Hannah was so distressed and how that deep distress drove her to pray fervently. (Do we have to care really deeply before we can start praying?)

Now read the Luke passage, and how all these different life journeys (of Zachariah, Joseph, Mary and Elizabeth) had been brought together by God leading each of them so that his plan of saving the world could be carried out. Split the group into four to prepare a 'story of my life so far' of each person involved, trying to imagine the way each might express him/herself. Then have spokespeople reading each life story out in turn.

Things to discuss

1 It was Hannah's deep pain which hurt her into praying so fervently. What does this suggest about the way we should pray, particularly in intercession?

2 Compare Mary's song of praise with Hannah's (in 1 Samuel 2).

THE MINISTRY
OF JESUS

Jesus teaches us about God

Thought for the day

Jesus teaches us by meeting us in our present situation and guiding us forward from there.

Things to read

Psalm 71
Job 28
Luke 6:20-38

Things to do

Aim: To celebrate the qualities of God's nature and face the challenge this gives us.

First play this game. One person thinks of someone in the group and everyone asks questions to try and guess who the mystery person is. They can be quite straightforward questions (e.g. 'Has he got black hair?') or for an older group the questions can be more subtle (e.g. 'What might his favourite drink be?' 'Where might she choose to go on holiday?') In the game we are working out someone's identity and character.

We can find out about God's character by reading about him, seeing him revealed in Jesus and through living in his company. Read the Old Testament passage together and then go straight on to the passage from Luke.

Make a list together of what God seems to be like, noting his righteousness and high expectations of our behaviour as well as his love and mercy. Discuss how easy it is to pick up on the parts we want to hear and disregard the truths about loving our enemies and not being complacent.

Help them to use the challenge of today's reading in tackling one particular area in their lives and bringing it under God's government.

Things to discuss

1 We know God is full of compassion and mercy, but what about the high standards of behaviour he expects?

2 How can we set about loving our enemies?

Christ can help us see

Thought for the day

Christ can heal us to wholeness, but only if we let him.

Things to read

Psalm 139:1-18
Numbers 21:4-9
John 9 (or 9:1-25)

Things to do

Aim: To look at both physical and spiritual blindness.

First read John 9 with people taking different parts. If the group enjoys acting, you could act the passage out as you read it. Then have a role-play involving the man himself, his parents and two friends he hasn't seen for a while and who want to know what has happened to him. De-role the actors (see Foreword) and follow with a role-play of some Pharisees talking to one of their friends who was visiting a relative when all this took place.

De-role again; talk together about the different kinds of blindness in the story and use the episode to challenge the state of our own 'sight'.

Things to discuss

1 The bronze snake was like the biting snakes but without the poisonous bite. Can you see the connection between this and the Son of Man being 'lifted up' on the cross?

2 Why do you think the blind man's parents, the religious leaders and the man himself all reacted as they did?

Jesus teaches in parables

Thought for the day

Jesus' glory is revealed in the parables he tells.

Things to read

Psalms 127, 128, 133
Isaiah 5:1-7
John 15:1-11

Things to do

Aim: To look at parables in layers.

First read the Old Testament vineyard story and the New Testament vine and branches passage. Set up a chart like this:

The vine and branches

and look for the different 'depths' or layers of meaning in the readings. Write them in.

Then in small groups, try making some composite pieces of writing which unlock the meaning of a parable. The word PARABLES is written down the side of the page and each letter becomes the beginning of a line. Here is an example to give you the idea:

Parables
Are a
Really
Amazing way of
Bringing out a message.
Listen and you will
Eventually discover a
Secret meaning.

The finished piece of writing can be shared and later written up and decorated and put in the parish paper.

Things to discuss

1 Look at some other parables of Jesus and discuss what their spiritual meanings are for you.

2 Sometimes Jesus wouldn't explain the stories he told until later. Why do you think he did this?

Jesus reveals a welcoming God

Thought for the day   God tells each of us our own story and loves us into his kingdom.

Things to read   Psalms 42, 43
1 Kings 10:1-13
John 4:1-26 or 1-42

Things to do   *Aim:* For them to know that they are specifically and personally known and loved.

Start with two people reading this short sketch.

Sentry: Halt! Who goes there?

Fred: It's me – Fred.

Sentry: Fred with the pony tail or bald Fred?

Fred: Fred with the pony tail. Can I come in?

Sentry: That depends.

Fred: Depends on what?

Sentry: Well, on what type of trainers you're wearing, for a start.

Fred: Is NIKE any good?

Sentry: Yes, NIKE's OK.

Fred: Well, they're not NIKE.

Sentry: What are they, then?

Fred: They were on special offer at Payless. Hang on, it says something on the sole . . . 'Made in Hong Kong'.

Sentry: Well, that's it, then. You can't come in if you're wearing those.

Fred: But my mum made me get these.

Sentry: Then you'd better make sure you get the right sort next time. Go and make yourself a bit more acceptable, for goodness' sake.

Talk together about how there are those who are only willing to be friends if we're wearing the right clothes, or have the right amount of intelligence or skill. And there are those whom we wouldn't trust with our personal ideas or worries because we know they might use the information against us. But if we know someone loves us, then we can trust them even with the things we are ashamed of, because we know they will try to understand, and our mistakes won't mean rejection.

Now read the passage from John, looking at how the woman might have felt about Jesus 'seeing right through her'. Bring out the point that Jesus knows us completely, and nothing at all is hidden from him. But he is also the God of love, so that knowledge is in safe hands, and he will always use it in the way that is best for us.

Things to Discuss

1 Go through the passage from John, covering up Jesus' replies as you go and thinking what you might expect them to be. What do Jesus' unexpected replies teach the woman, and what do they teach us?

2 Do we question Jesus in our prayer and during our lives? Perhaps we don't often become aware of his voice because we censor what we consider unsuitable things to talk over with him.

Grounded in God

Thought for the day   What we are determines how we fruit.

Things to read   Psalm 73
Proverbs 8:1-17
Luke 6:39-end

Things to do   *Aim:* For them to understand the sense of building their lives on Jesus.

Start by giving playing cards to everyone and letting them make card houses, some on smooth, firm bases and some on rough, wobbly ones. Whose can withstand the most blowing?
  Now read the passage from Luke together, and look at why Jesus was so angry with the 'blind guides'. Talk about what it means to them to have their lives built on the foundation of faith in God, including the difficulties this may cause as well as the blessings. Plan a youth event which will reach their contemporaries who do not yet know Jesus as a living person.

Things to discuss   1 In what ways were the religious teachers of Jesus' time being blind guides? In what ways are religious people sometimes blind guides today?

2 To what extent do we have free choice, bearing in mind the factors of upbringing, genes, circumstances, etc.?

God's upside-down wisdom

Thought for the day   God's wisdom turns our priorities upside-down.

Things to read   Psalm 19
2 Samuel 9
Matthew 6:19-end

Things to do   *Aim:* For them to look at the practicalities of what Jesus' teaching implies.

First split into groups of two or three and make a list of the things people their age worry about, and what they think the very old and the very young worry about. Share these ideas in the full group. Talk about the value of a certain amount of anxiety, but the imprisoning effect on our lives that constant worrying has.

Now read the passage from Matthew, looking at Jesus' teaching about this. They may immediately respond to some of it; other parts may seem foolhardy or difficult to practise. Follow the progress of the discussion on a flip-chart. Lead the discussion into the area of our responsibility for providing for those who lack food and clothing, and work on planning an event to help in this.

Things to discuss   1 Why do people worry? Why does being a Christian make any difference?

2 How can we live out this gospel in (though not necessarily of) a materialistic society?

Christ transforms suffering

Thought for the day

Being a Christian doesn't take all the suffering away, but transforms our way of dealing with it.

Things to read

Psalms 130, 137:1-6
Isaiah 49: 13-23
Matthew 11:20-end

Things to do

Aim: For them to look at what Jesus offers, and why his offer is often refused.

Read the passage from Matthew straight through, then concentrate on the end part first. It is important that everyone knows how a yoke worked, and understands that it eased the burden to be yoked up with a strong, experienced ox.

Talk together about how Jesus' invitation works.

How do we know God makes our loads easier to carry?

Does the yoke image suggest that he takes the load away from us, or shares it with us?

How much of our load is the load itself, and how much our feelings of grumpiness about having to carry it, and what does Jesus do about this if we let him?

It is important that doubts and questions are aired, and that the conversation is open and honest; there may well be times when we wish Jesus would do things differently! If our young people are going to deepen their faith they need to know the implications of choosing to accept Jesus' invitation for themselves, and not do so just because we have told them to.

Now go back to the earlier part of the reading. If Jesus did all those amazing things, why wasn't he believed? Why don't people today take up his offer of an easier life, when it sounds like an obvious good bargain? Keep track of ideas raised, and include the point that we keep wanting to go our own way, and we can't do that and stay yoked with Jesus at the same time. Yokes are not that elastic. Have a time of prayer for desperate situations and people who are heavily burdened in various different ways. Choose one to pray for each day during the week. If there is time, finish with a go at three-legged walking to experience the need to choose to walk in step with the one to whom you are yoked.

Things to discuss

1 Why do you think that people who lived in the area where Jesus lived and worked didn't believe, in spite of all those miracles? What makes us sceptical and prejudiced?

2 In what ways have you found Jesus' burden to be light?

Glory on a donkey

Thought for the day

The King of glory rides on a donkey into Jerusalem.

Things to read

Psalms 61, 62
Jeremiah 7:1-11 or Exodus 11
Luke 19:29-end

Things to do

Aim: To bring the events of the readings to life for them.

If you have access to one of the videos about Jesus' life, show them the section of the entry into Jerusalem and the cleaning-up of the temple. Or they can act this out, with everyone involved either as vendors or crowd members. Afterwards, talk together about how different people felt when Jesus came in and started protesting, overturning tables and so on. If possible, join in with an all-age procession, leading the singing or dancing for one or two of the songs.

Things to discuss

1   Our society believes in allowing everyone the freedom to do more or less what feels right for them, so long as it doesn't interfere with others. Where does this view start to clash with Christian values and beliefs?

2   Why did Jesus feel so angry with the money changers in the temple, and why do you think he decided to deal so forcibly with them?

Jesus, the friend of sinners

Thought for the day

If you are a sinner, then Jesus considers you a friend.

Things to read

Psalms 56, 57
Jeremiah 33:1-11
Luke 7:36-8:3

Things to do

Aim: To explore the quality of God's friendship.

Read the Old Testament passage together and think about how God was befriending Jeremiah here. Then read the New Testament passage, if possible from the Dramatised Bible.

Go through the different characters in turn, looking at what each was thinking. When you get to Jesus, think about how he felt towards each of the other characters – bearing in mind his love and affection for each of them.

Now try looking with Jesus' eyes at various people in different situations of conflict or misunderstanding. Look at one international situation, one national and one very local. How will Jesus' personal and forgiving love, coupled with perfect knowledge and understanding of backgrounds, affect the way we respond to the people in these situations?

Things to discuss

1 How does Jesus' attitude to sinners suggest we ought to behave towards those whose behaviour we disapprove of?

2 Do we let God completely forgive us, or do we tend to punish ourselves as if this will help?

Jesus' 'simple' way of love

Thought for the day

Jesus meets us where we are and leads us forward.

Things to read

Psalm 71
Deuteronomy 5:1-21
Luke 13:22-end

Things to do

Aim: To explore how Jesus taught the 'simple' way of love.

Look together at the ten commandments, noticing what the priorities are and linking them with Jesus' summary of them: love God and love your neighbour as yourself. Then read the teaching in Luke about the narrow gateway, emphasising that there is only room for us as we are, and no way we can get through while carrying all the clutter of possessions, bitterness, an inflated sense of our own importance and so on.

Have some large bulky bundles and discuss what labels they may have. Pray together for discernment to see what luggage we have collected which has become too important to us and is preventing us from living God's way.

Draw a poster for the church notice board (*not* one near the entrance!) which shows a narrow opening with a notice hung up beside it saying, 'Please leave all luggage at the door.'

Things to discuss

1 How is Jesus' summary of the law similar to the ten commandments and how is it different?

2 What might we need to put down, as individuals and as a church, if we are to fit through the narrow gateway?

NEW LIFE IN CHRIST

Christ in glory

Thought for the day

Having paid for our freedom with his life, Jesus our Saviour enters into the full glory to which he is entitled.

Things to read

Psalm 108, 110
Isaiah 65:17–end
Revelation 5

Things to do

Aim: To help them understand what the Ascension was and what it means.

Start by having a whistle-stop tour through all the accounts of the Ascension, noting what features are similar in each and what different details each supply.

Try to glean from the accounts the important things which are being said – that Jesus is victorious; he has won the battle against sin and death and is given authority to reign. Then consider these questions:

Why didn't Jesus go straight up to heaven when he rose from the dead?

Why didn't he make sure everybody saw him?

I suggest that rather than working as a whole group for this part, you have people in small groups of two or three, so as to enable everyone to join in. Share some of the discussion points in the whole group afterwards.

Things to discuss

1 Can we hasten the coming of the kingdom? If so, how?

2 Does our world show any indications that the kingdom of God is advancing?

Celebrate the Good News

Thought for the day	Death cannot hold the Lord of life. New life for him means new life for all who believe in Christ.
Things to read	Psalms 113, 114, 117 Isaiah 12 Romans 6:3-14
Things to do	Aim: To celebrate the good news of resurrection. You will need some balloons, acetate pens (or others that work on balloons) and, if possible, a helium balloon filler. Failing this, strong lungs will do nicely. If they have not just heard it read in the church, read the Easter story from one of the gospels, keeping the Romans passage until the discussion later on. Then ask them to write 'Jesus is alive' on the balloons and decorate them so they can blow them up and give them out to people at the end of the service.
Things to discuss	1 Read the Romans passage: what does Paul mean when he says, 'You are not under law, but under grace'? 2 What about Christians who have been brought up in the faith and can't remember a time before they were baptised?

Children in God's family

Thought for the day	Whatever our age or marital status, we are all children in God's family, brothers and sisters bound together by love.

Things to read

Psalm 103
Genesis 47:1-12
Colossians 3:12-21

Things to do

Aim: To see how one man was becoming a nation, as God had promised, and to look at family life.

Use a family tree chart to trace the way God was making a family grow into a nation. Then read the Genesis passage together, with different voices for the speaking parts. Notice how Joseph, Jacob and the brothers act towards one another and towards the king of Egypt. What has the family learnt through their experiences?

Now get into small groups and make a list of the plus and the minus side of family life. After a few minutes, gather their thoughts onto a chart.

Read the passage from Colossians to see what advice Paul gives about living in harmony with others, and see how this could apply to the list of good and bad aspects of family life. Have a time of prayer for those finding home life particularly difficult at the moment, and those who are separated from their families through war or famine.

Things to discuss

1 Notice how the very elderly Jacob takes it upon himself to bless the mighty king of Egypt, even though his own status is only that of nomadic shepherd. What is our society's attitude to the elderly? What about our church community? Any changes needed?

2 If Paul were writing today, what do you think he might say to us about family life?

Citizens of heaven

Thought for the day

Heaven is our home.

Things to read

Psalm 89:1-18
Ezekiel 11:14-21
Hebrews 13:1-21

Things to do

Aim: For them to look at the implications of being citizens of heaven.

First look at some local road maps, and ask them to work in twos or threes, finding the way to various places and jotting down the route. Then the instructions are swapped, so that they have to find their way from each other's directions.

Now read the passage from Ezekiel, and talk about the way God calls his people back home from far away. It isn't just a physical distance, but a spiritual one as well. Explain how Jesus is the way for us to travel home to God, and because he paid the price of death he has opened up the possibility of heaven to us. We are citizens of heaven, and need to behave like that on our journey home.

Now read the passage from Hebrews and look at the kind of behaviour which does and doesn't seem appropriate for sons and daughters of the living God. Talk over any they want to look at more carefully, and end with a time of prayer.

Things to discuss

1 Through the generations the Church wobbles its way, trying to keep its balance between condemnation and forgiveness. Where do you think we are at the moment, and what attitudes need changing?

2 Although the kingdom is other-worldly, and to do with what happens spiritually, it is also a social gospel. Why are both important?

Values determine actions

Thought for the day   Our fundamental values determine the fruit we bear.

Things to read   Psalm 73
Numbers 11:16-17, 24-29
Acts 8:4-25

Things to do   *Aim:* For them to explore the way our deeply held values show in how we act.

First read the passage from Numbers, and pick out the qualities of Moses' character which are shown up clearly by his reaction to Joshua's righteous indignation. Then look at the account of Philip's ministry in Samaria, and the way Simon reacted to the coming of the Holy Spirit. What does his reaction show us about his values, in spite of the fact that he has listened to Philip's teaching and been baptised?

Work on the two accounts using role-plays in small groups, either to be a chat in the wilderness involving Joshua, one of the seventy men and an onlooker; or a chat in Samaria involving a recently baptised Christian, Simon and Philip.

Remember to de-role the people taking part (see Foreword) after the role-play is over.

Things to discuss   1 How do you think we can train ourselves to be less possessive of our status, our ideas or our 'territory'?

2 Sometimes we put people on pedestals because we admire them. Having read the passage from Numbers, what dangers do you think there are in doing this? Is there anything we could do to protect young heroes and heroines from such dangers?

Not just patched but renewed

Thought for the day   In Jesus we are not just patched up but made new.

Things to read   Psalm 77
Isaiah 43:14-44:5
Mark 2:18-3:6

Things to do   *Aim:* For them to see how lives are changed and made new in Christ.

Briefly explain how the people of Israel were in exile, having broken faith with God time and again. Now God speaks to them through his prophet, Isaiah.

Read this passage together, and then go to Mark. Talk about how Jesus was fulfilling the promise the people had received in exile, and yet he wasn't easily accepted by his own people. List some of their ideas as to why his behaviour seems to have been angering them.

Now either watch a short clip from a video, or browse through information books in small groups so as to make a display of people whose lives have been completely turned around and made new through getting involved with Jesus.

There are lots of people to choose from, and you may have people in your congregation with stories to tell. Or look at some of these: Francis and Clare, Father Damian, Jacquie Pullinger, Nicky Cruz, Mother Teresa, Corrie Ten Boom.

Things to discuss   1 In what sense does Jesus teach according to the law of Moses, and in what sense does he make all things new?

2 Are there any of our traditions or habits which need renewing, discarding and/or fulfilling?

True freedom

Thought for the day

True freedom neither means doing what you like nor being trapped by someone else's sin.

Things to read

Psalms 42, 43
Ezekiel 18:1-4, 19-end
Romans 14:1-15:3

Things to do

Aim: To explore the ways in which the Romans passage challenges our behaviour.

Begin by explaining how the old Jewish laws had said there were some foods which Jews shouldn't eat. Some Christian Jews did not understand that as Christians they were now free to eat all foods. Now read the passage from Paul's letter to the Christians in Rome, noticing how he reacts to their problems.

Give out a questionnaire something like this (see below), but make sure it is relevant to your group's experience, and ask them to work on this in small groups. Afterwards, have a discussion on the answers chosen, and pray together about any challenges or needs which have arisen.

QUESTIONNAIRE

Answer each question: yes, perhaps or no.

1 Would you buy something from a shop which sells a lot of New Age things and/or anti-Christian material?

2 You are a vegetarian and get invited out to a meal which turns out to contain meat. Do you:
   a) eat it out of politeness
   b) refuse to eat anything and grumble at your host
   c) eat the vegetables and leave the meat?

3 Some people at your church refuse to clap along to a song in church and you catch their disapproving look. Do you:
   a) clap louder than ever through every hymn to show how free in the Spirit you are
   b) clap discreetly and feel guilty
   c) continue as you are but make a point of being friendly to them after the service?

4 At camp another Christian kneels to pray at night and gets teased. You are used to praying in bed, so no one knows you are praying. The following night, do you:

   a) pray in bed as usual

   b) kneel down as the other person is

   c) join in the teasing?

5 You give up chocolate for Lent and a friend from a different tradition thinks the idea is medieval. Do you:

   a) have a heated argument in front of non-Christian friends

   b) go back to eating chocolate for a quiet life whenever your friend is around

   c) recognise that you hold the important things in common and it isn't worth arguing about such matters?

Things to discuss

1 Religious wars are often what put peace-loving people off organised religion. What has gone wrong to bring about a religious war?

2 If we seriously decide to pray 'Thy kingdom come, thy will be done', what attitudes and behaviour might we need to change

   a) in ourselves

   b) in our local worshipping community

   c) in our particular church tradition?

Avoiding hypocrisy and false piety

Thought for the day   If we really understood God's law it would drive us weeping to his feet.

Things to read   Psalm 119:41-56
Nehemiah 8:1-12
Luke 11:37-end

Things to do   *Aim:* To explore the growth of false piety and ways to avoid hypocrisy.

First explain how the Pharisees had originally formed to protect the Jewish faith from corruption at a time when there was a very real danger of this happening. By Jesus' time they had got somewhat carried away with what they were preserving, and were now more concerned with the outer rituals and signs than the real thing.

Now read the passage from Luke together and think how the Pharisees, who still considered themselves guardians of the faith, would have felt about Jesus. List the things that might anger them, and the things that concerned Jesus as he tried to break through the hard crust of tradition and free the living faith that was trapped inside.

In twos and threes talk as Pharisees about Jesus when he's out of earshot. (Incidentally, Paul was a Pharisee, and we can see in his writings what happened once he realised that Jesus was the key person in the very faith he was determined to guard.)

De-role the players (see Foreword) and take a look at your own faith and parish, checking areas where a 'back to basics' session may be needed.

Things to discuss   1 How can we make sure that people really understand God's word in a way which guides them to realise God's love for them?

2 The Pharisees had begun by zealously protecting the true faith, and upholding it against dangerous outside influences. Can you see how this might have turned into the false piety we see here? And are there any danger signs for the Church today?

Revolutionary new life

Thought for the day
New life means revolution, and it can only happen through God's freely given power.

Things to read
Psalms 11, 20
Micah 3:5-end
Matthew 5:27-end

Things to do
Aim: To explore the teaching in Matthew 5 with reference to their own lives and decisions.

Start by reading the passage from Matthew 5, looking up the Old Testament references as you go. They are:

Matthew 5:27 – Exodus 20:14
Matthew 5:31 – Deuteronomy 24:1
Matthew 5:33 – Leviticus 19:12
Matthew 5:38 – Exodus 21:24
Leviticus 24:20
Deuteronomy 19:21
Matthew 5:43 – Leviticus 19:18

Make it clear that Jesus was not smashing the old law, but explaining its true meaning; he was helping his listeners to get at the spirit of the law, rather than the letter as the Pharisees' teaching tended to do.
Go through the sections one by one, jotting down their ideas about what the spirit of these laws might be in our own lives.

Things to discuss
1 In the Micah passage, what made God especially disturbed by the prophets, leaders and judges?

2 Do you find that Jesus' teaching on how we should live seems excessively strict? How on earth does he expect us to keep to his rulings?

God in us: Christ's risen life

Thought for the day

In Jesus we see the face of God, and his risen life enables him to live in us.

Things to read

Psalms 30, 48
Deuteronomy 11:1-15
2 Corinthians 4:5-end

Things to do

Aim: To help them see examples of how faith in the living Jesus changes people's lives.

If you have some new Christians in the church, invite them along to tell their story; not that older Christians couldn't do it, too, of course, but often new Christians are especially excited about it all. Or you can use excerpts from autobiographies, such as Nicky Cruz's story in *Run, Baby, Run*.

Let it also be a question time to air their concerns about their own faith or lack of it, or difficulties their non-Christian friends have with believing in a real, living Jesus. End with a time of expectant prayer.

Things to discuss

1 How can we get to know Jesus in a personal way?

2 What about the dark or foggy times when we aren't aware of Jesus' presence?

FAITH, TRUST, HOPE

God's call and Abraham's faith

Thought for the day   God chooses Abraham; Abraham responds in faith.

Things to read   Psalms 32, 36
Isaiah 55
Galatians 3:1-14

Things to do   *Aim:* To explore how God draws near to us and we to him.

Have ready some advertisements of expensive items from a mail order catalogue. Choose things your group would probably like to have but can't afford. Also, have several calculators available.

In small groups, ask them to work out how long it would take them to earn enough to buy a chosen item by saving pocket money/paper round money, etc. For some things, they'd probably be too old to enjoy them before they'd managed to earn enough.

Now read the Galatians passage. We can sometimes get into the 'learning mode' with God, but Paul is saying it's more like some generous person offering to give us, as a free present, what we're struggling hard to earn.

Where does the 'faith' part come in?

When we're offered a present, we can choose whether or not to receive it. God offers us his love and forgiveness and constant 'presence' but that grace is only able to work in our lives if we receive it in faith, open it up, get to know it and use it daily.

Things to discuss   1 Earning seems better to us than freely receiving. How can we change this unhelpful attitude?

2 Why does Paul call the Galatians 'foolish'?

Building up defences against temptation

Thought for the day

We need to build up our defences against temptation.

Things to read

Psalm 119:9-24
Exodus 17:1-13
Matthew 26:1-30

Things to do

Aim: To tackle the area of our (sometimes false) assumptions about God.

Begin by drawing attention to some of the tragedies which make people think there can't be a loving God or he wouldn't allow such suffering. Then read the first part of the Old Testament passage, where the people feel in real danger of dying out there in the desert with no water. Now read on to see how Moses reacts instead of being disillusioned. Break off to discuss the importance of doing this in our times of panic and suffering, even when there seems no hope at all. Finally, look at the outcome of God responding to Moses' correct assumption that God cares and will provide.

Make a chart headed: 'How do we know God is concerned with the welfare of his world?' Discuss this, jotting down the thoughts that are raised. Think about how we might help someone who is at the 'grumbling' stage to understand God better.

Things to discuss

1 How do we know for certain that God is concerned for our eternal well-being?

2 If we really trust God's goodness, how will that affect our response to suffering?

The cost of discipleship

Thought for the day

Following Christ is not always a comfortable place to be.

Things to read

Psalm 119:73-88
Amos 3
Matthew 26:31-56

Things to do

Aim: To help them be aware of the unhealthy state of society and its expectations.

First explain the background to Amos, so that they can hear the prophecy in context. Then read it together, explaining the meaning where necessary as you go.

Make a list of some of the situations which Amos might speak out against in our society, our era and our church. Put a star by any they feel could be changed by popular opinion.

Put a circle by any they reckon most people go along with because they want to stay out of trouble.

Put a triangle by any that people have protested about and ended up getting into trouble.

Now have a look at any conclusions the markings suggest.

Pray together for the courage to stand out even when at risk.

Things to discuss

1 What do you think Amos might thunder against in our church and society?

2 Are there any areas in our lives where we hang back from acting as Christians for fear of the consequences?

Jesus, the unexpected Messiah

Thought for the day

Christ had to suffer in order to rescue us.

Things to read

Psalm 119:105-120
Job 2
Matthew 26:57-end

Things to do

Aim: To look at the reasons for Jesus' suffering.

Begin with this game. Explain that you and your accomplice have a code and they are going to try and crack it. If they think they understand it, then they can have a go at decoding the next message. Carry on until everyone has sussed out the code. This is the code: for each letter of the word, you say something beginning with the letter (such as 'Could we put it here? . . . At the corner, I think . . . That's it', which turns out to be CAT). The misleading part is that at the same time you are carefully placing a knife and fork in various ways, so that people expect this to be the code, rather than the things you are saying. In fact, the knife and fork are of no significance at all.

Now read the gospel passage together, with a small group acting it out if that method suits them.

Talk about how our expectations in the code put us off understanding for a while, and how the religious leaders' expectations of the way the Messiah would behave effectively blocked their acceptance of him when he came.

Things to discuss

1 There are many reasons why Jesus was not received when he came to live among us, in spite of all the love he showed. Why do people not receive him – now as well as then?

2 What similarities can you see between the Job story and this episode in Peter's life?

Enduring and persevering

Thought for the day   If we endure, we shall reign with him.

Things to read   Psalm 51
Jeremiah 38:1-13
James 1:1-15

Things to do   *Aim:* For them to look at ways of enduring and persevering when it is difficult.

Start by reading the story of Jeremiah in the well and his rescue. Talk about times when their friends have managed to get them out of a tight spot, or times when they have felt abandoned, as Jeremiah must have felt in the mud at the bottom of the muddy well. (They may remember that Joseph was also dumped in a well.)

Now read the passage from James, picking out his words which link up with Matthew 5:11-12. Talk about our different strategies for keeping going when things are difficult, and list the ideas so everyone can learn from one another. Look, too, at the way Peter managed to walk on the water – and what made him start sinking (Matthew 14:29). Have a time of prayer for those who are enduring persecution and hardship for Jesus at the moment; Amnesty International has special details of specific people to whom you can send encouragement, and letters asking for their release.

Things to discuss   1 Could you share with one another the times when God has ministered to you in the middle of a difficult time, to enable you to carry on?

2 Have you noticed any difference in the way you cope with things going wrong if they happen because of your belief in Jesus, rather than through your own sin or foolishness?

We can rely on God

Thought for the day	In his own good time, God is drawing all things to perfect completion.

Things to read

Psalms 23, 24 or 78:1-24
Job 4:1 and 5:1-16
Hebrews 10:19-end

Things to do

Aim: For them to know that with God nothing is impossible, and our hope in him is never disappointed.

Bring along a photo album of pictures which include church events through the years, or family events of some of those in the group. When you have all had a good laugh, talk about the way a community builds up its love and commitment by all the things it has laughed and struggled through together. In God's family it is just the same. At every anniversary of the great events of their history the people of Israel would relive the way God had lifted them out of trouble.

As Christians we remember the main events of Jesus' life, death and resurrection each year, because they have changed our outlook and given us hope.

Read Psalm 78:1-24 together, and then the passage from Hebrews. Finish with a prayer and worship time, reaffirming their trust in God, and welcoming his power into their lives.

Things to discuss

1 So many people are paralysed or distorted through fear of one sort or another. So many aggressive, violent people have fear in their eyes. Is there any way that we can speak to this fear the word of God's peace so that they understand?

2 It is not unusual to find young people drifting away from the church a year or two after having made a commitment to Christ. What might be the reasons for this, and what do you think we could do as a church to prevent the 'soul drain'?

God or self: our choice

Thought for the day

You cannot live with self and God both at the centre of your life; you will have to choose between them.

Things to read

Psalms 42, 43
Proverbs 14:31-15:17
James 4:31-5:11

Things to do

Aim: For them to recognise the choice they can make, and the consequences of that choice.

Begin with a game involving choice, such as the 'Stone, paper, scissors' game, or 'Forfeits' based on spinning a coin. Some choices we make in life are quite arbitrary, and we have no idea whether we will be choosing profitably or not. Many people love the excitement they get from this kind of choice, and gambling is addictive.

Other choices are based on assessing the situation and reasoning your next move – like choosing your secondary school, deciding how to play the next shot, or deciding which socks to buy.

Some choices are really important, because they affect a large part of your life – choosing who to marry, or whether to go for promotion. The most important decision of all is the one that affects us not only in this life, but after death as well. Are we going to choose God or self to reign in our lives?

Now read the passage from James' letter, looking at the kind of differences this choice makes in our behaviour. If we want the world to be a better, happier place because we have lived, we will have to make a conscious decision not to have self at the centre of our lives.

Things to discuss

1 When does it seem like a straight choice between God and self, and when is the distinction blurred?

2 Should Christians get involved with social and political issues? To what extent should we work for Christian morality in a largely non-Christian society?

What is faith?

Thought for the day

Commit your ways to God; he promises to look after your needs and he will not let you down.

Things to read

Psalm 37:1-22
Job 23:1-12
2 Corinthians 1:1-22

Things to do

Aim: To help them understand what faith is.

Begin by reading the passages from Job and Corinthians. In small groups, find two different dimensions of faith from these passages and then discuss the findings in the full group.

Look at these images and see in what ways they are right, and in what ways they don't give the true picture.

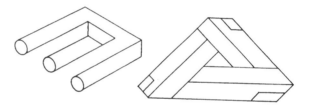

Then go back into small groups to write a few words to explain what faith really is, and share these definitions in the full group again.

Things to discuss

1 How would you describe faith? How does it link with such things as trust, wishes, optimism or brainwashing?

2 What do you think Paul means when he talks about God giving us both suffering and consolation? Have you ever found that times of great stress have actually been learning times when you have understood more of God's love and increased your faith?

Exploring the mystery of God

Thought for the day   Work for God's glory, not your own.

Things to read   Psalms 91, 93
                            Judges 7:1-8, 19-23
                            John 7:1-24

Things to do   *Aim:* To explore the way God leads us 'mysteriously' but we can trust him to know what's best.

Beforehand, prepare a trail of clues which make up a message. Use this one (NIV) or one of your own.

- Psalm 20:7 Some – – – – –
- Genesis 1:1 In the beginning – – –
- Exodus 2:3 coated it with tar – – –
- John 2:5 His mother said to the servants – – – – – – – – – –
  – – – – – – – – – –

Point out that if they had stopped half way they wouldn't have found the answer to the puzzle. If we stop listening out for God in our lives he won't be able to complete the excellent plan he has for us and all those he was planning to bless along the way by our action.

Read the Gideon story together, checking each instruction to see how Gideon's faith kept him listening, even when God wasn't suggesting the accepted way of going on.

Then read the passage from John and notice Jesus' obedience which kept him alertly listening, so that he spoke and behaved in harmony with his Father, and not as the teachers and experts expected him to behave. Make a space for a discussion/question time of areas they may be exploring in their own lives – such as how we are to be sure what is God's voice and what is just ourselves; how God actually communicates with us; a natural wariness of it all being a con and so on. Finish with a time of quiet prayer and music.

Things to discuss   1 What hints do we have of Gideon's faith in this story? What about us – do we prefer to see the end before we start to follow? Why does God show us only a bit at a time?

                            2 What was it in Jesus that made the people love him and their teachers find him so threatening? Are we, as a church and as individuals, ever threatening to others through our disobedience to God's will?

A Christian response to suffering

Thought for the day

Being a Christian doesn't take all the suffering away, but transforms our way of dealing with it.

Things to read

Psalms 130, 137:1-6
2 Kings 19:8-19
Acts 16:16-end

Things to do

Aim: To explore the way Christians respond to suffering.

First read the Old Testament passage, and share times when they have had very frightening or disappointing letters. Suggest they try Hezekiah's idea. Look at the stages of Hezekiah's prayer, too, so that it can become a model or pattern for them.

Then look at the Paul and Silas story, having different people to read different characters in it. Pause at the point they are thrown into prison and talk about how they might have felt at this point, and then go on to read about the way they dealt with the situation. We can do the same, odd though it may feel at first. To get the sense of praying in various situations, make a praise trail round the premises, where labels are put up on places such as the rubbish dump, a dark, crowded cupboard, the loo, a bramble patch and so on. The labels suggest situations which are very unpleasant or worse, such as 'Bitter disappointment', 'Unfair criticism', 'Severe irritation' or 'Personal failure', but it's best if you make your own up so that they are particularly relevant to your group. Then people can walk round and praise God in each setting, in practice for the real thing.

Things to discuss

1 Do we still behave as if this life isn't the end, or have we lost that abandoned, reckless joy of these early Christians?

2 Can we just decide to care less about the things that go wrong, or does there have to be a deeper change of priorities in our whole personality before our behaviour can change?

Signs of glory

Thought for the day   God reveals himself through signs and wonders.

Things to read
Psalms 135, 136
Isaiah 26:1-9
John 4:43-end

Things to do
Aim: To help them see how God reveals his glory in signs.

You will need a collection of optical illusions, like those shown below.

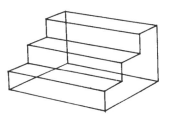

Start by looking at the pictures until you can see them in both forms, then work out a jigsaw together. Point out that as you get more clues it gets easier to understand the picture. Think also of 'Blind Date' where, in a few questions, the aim is to reveal enough of the characters of the possibles to judge their suitability for a date!

Since God is personal, we will need to get to know him as we do human people – through our conversations and quiet times together, through seeing the way he thinks and acts. Look together at John 1, where John claims that the Word of God came and walked about amongst us. His evidence is that they could see his glory, full of grace and truth. Explain how John then goes on to record a series of seven signs of the glory which support Jesus' claims, including today's healing. Take a whistle-stop tour through John to notice the other six:

2:1-12 (water into new wine); 4:43-54 (feeding the five thousand and then walking on the water); 5 (healing of the lame man); 9 (blind man sees while the sighted shut out the light); 11 (Lazarus raised to life). Make a note of each as you go through, so that they can look at the overall picture.

If there is time, share evidence that members of the group have seen in their own lives which shows that God is living and active.

Things to discuss

1 We can't kid ourselves into faith, however much we strain ourselves, because faith is a gift freely given. But how can we prepare the ground for faith to grow?

2 What signs did Jesus show in his life which led his disciples to believe that he was the promised one from God?

Keep alert

Thought for the day

Keep alert, because much is demanded of those to whom much is entrusted.

Things to read

Psalm 18:1-32
Isaiah 1:1-20
Luke 12:35-48

Things to do

Aim: To explore the practicalities of keeping alert for when Jesus comes.

Read together the passage from Luke 12. Then give out copies of this script to act out.

WHAT'S IN STORE

Characters: Manager, Assistant, Customer, Boss.

Provide a jacket and tie for the manager, various items of the store's produce and some authentic cardboard cartons. The manager and shop assistant are moving cartons from one place in the shop to another.

Manager: Easy does it, Fred.

Assistant: Yes, sir.

Manager: Always bend your knees, rather than your back.

Assistant: Yes, sir.

Manager: I take my responsibilities seriously, you know; and as shop assistant your back is one of my heavy responsibilities.

Assistant: Yes, sir. These chocolate and nut cookies weigh a ton, don't they, sir?

Manager: Ah yes, more heavy responsibilities the boss left me with, eh . . . ha, ha!

Customer: Hallo, Harold! The boss gone away and left you in charge, has he? How about a packet of chocolate and nut cookies for friendship's sake? I'll buy you a pint this evening at the Crown.

Manager: You owe me a pint as it is, you old skinflint! And anyway, what do you think the boss would think if he came back and found me dishing out his stock? He's left me in charge because he reckons I'll look after things properly for him.

Customer: I don't think you'll see the boss in a hurry. He's lazing in the sun somewhere, I expect. Anyway, I'll have some chewing gum.

He buys chewing gum, thanks the manager and leaves.

Manager: What's that grinding noise, Fred?

Assistant: That's my stomach, sir. It seems a long time since breakfast.

He strokes one of the packets of cookies.

Manager: Yes, I'm rather peckish myself. Oh, come on, let's split a packet of these between us! Bill's probably right – the boss won't be back yet.

They do so, and start eating.

Boss comes in and is amazed at what is going on. Then he coughs to get their attention.

Boss: So this is the man who was so sure I could trust him, is it?

Manager: *[Trying to hide biscuits]* Mr. Taylor! . . . I wasn't expecting you!

Boss: Evidently. Mr. Woodman . . .

Manager: Yes, sir?

Boss: You're fired.

Ask the group to list suggestions for practical ways to stay alert and avoid falling into temptation.

Things to discuss

1 Obedience is something most of us find very hard. How is it linked to selfishness and what factors make it easier/ more difficult for us to do?

2 When is obedience a matter of life and death? How can we practise obedience in little ways so we're ready for the Big Event?

Discerning the truth

Thought for the day   God's wisdom is that of a living, powerful creator.

Things to read   Psalm 119:121-136
Jeremiah 10:1-16
1 Timothy 3:4-4:10

Things to do   *Aim:* To help them discern the true and living God, rather than false images of him.

Look at the Bible readings suggested, comparing the images people worship with the power and beauty of the living God. Sing some songs of worship and praise, such as *I will declare, Majesty, You are beautiful beyond description, Father, we love you, Living Lord,* or whatever are appropriate. Get each person or small group to take one description of God and write it so that it expresses the meaning. These can be displayed through the year on the church notice board.

Things to discuss   1 Why do humans try to manipulate the living God into a false image?

2 What marks out worshippers of the true God?

Choosing and Responding

Thought for the day	God chooses Abraham; Abraham responds in faith.
Things to read	Psalms 32, 36 Genesis 18:1-10 Romans 9:1-13
Things to do	*Aim:* To explore choosing and responding.

Read the Abraham passage together, imagining how Abraham might have felt at the news. Think about how his reaction would depend on the relationship he already had with God and his experience of God so far in his life.

Now get everyone talking and chatting while one person has to try and tell them something. If the messenger can't make himself heard, he may try speaking more loudly. If that fails, he may go round trying to get each one's attention and even then they may not listen.

Notice how Abraham had already settled himself ready to listen to his guests, so he heard the message clearly. Unless we deliberately set out to listen to what God is saying, we may well miss what he is trying to tell us. When we are in tune with God speaking to us through the Bible, through other people, through events in our lives and so on, we are still free to respond positively or negatively, as we wish. Pray together that you will all be able to recognise God's voice better, and be brave enough to go along with what he says.

Things to discuss

1 When we make ourselves available, God can use us – but on his terms. Do we really believe him enough to do this seriously, or do we really doubt that God can actually do things in our lives?

2 How honest are we with God about the things we feel he might be disappointed / hurt to discover?

TEMPTATION, SIN, FORGIVENESS

God saves

Thought for the day
Sin destroys us; God can save us.

Things to read
Psalm 25
Jeremiah 17:5-14
Romans 5:12-end

Things to do
Aim: To understand the peace of mind which comes from trusting God.

Read Jeremiah together. Discuss what it means in practice to trust in human resources. Jot down all the ideas on a board or flip-chart. Now give the group some situations, such as:

> a school leaver can't get a job and likes dressing well
> your best friend has moved away
> Mum and Dad have split up and you don't get on with Dad's girlfriend.

Talk about each situation, seeing how it will look and how you might act if you are trusting in people/trusting in God. Make notes of people's ideas under the two headings.

Things to discuss
1 Looking at our society/our world, what would you think it was trusting in?

2 What would change in our society if people really trusted in God?

God saves and uses the leftovers

Thought for the day

God preserves a remnant, whatever the surrounding evil.

Things to read

Psalm 147
Genesis 6:5-end
1 Peter 3:8-end

Things to do

Aim: To explore where rules work and fail, and discover what rule we really need.

Have some appropriate rules written out to start discussion on why rules are necessary. Look at the irritating truth that one person's selfishness can make life tedious for everyone else. Look at the way human nature tends towards self-gratification unless love is involved.

Read together the Genesis passage, then try a lucky-dip role-play – put the following characters on folded slips of paper in a hat and each person takes one. They take up their positions and argue it out!

The characters:
   Noah (a friendly farmer who wants everyone to be happy)
   Mrs. Noah (fed up with the hard work and grieving for her drowning friends)
   Shem (rather bossy and wanting to get the animals organised)
   Ham (happy to be on board as long as he doesn't have to do anything)
   Esther (finding it hard to swim but refusing to be rescued)
   A giraffe (frightened of going into the ark)
   Rebecca (too engrossed with the way the water is affecting her hairstyle to hear an invitation to be rescued)
   Jo and Ruth (still arguing over whose fault it was that their fire had gone out)

Be sure to de-role the actors (see Forword) at the end – especially important in this case since there may have been considerable conflict 'in role'.

Things to discuss

1 What do you think would happen if there were no laws or rules in society? What about in a Christian community?

2 What does this tell us about human nature?

Preparing the way for salvation

Thought for the day	Through his messengers, God prepares the way for salvation.
Things to read	Psalm 80 1 Kings 18:17-39 Luke 3:1-20

Things to do

Aim: To help them see the relevance of John the Baptist's teaching in their own lives.

Begin by asking them to line themselves up in order of height, then in order of shoe size, then by the number of beans they can hold in one hand (dried or baked if you are feeling adventurous or gross). You will find that the way they line up varies according to the standard or yardstick.

Now read the Luke passage together, asking them to look out for the standard John the Baptist wanted them to use in getting their lives lined up. Keep note of the suggestions made after the reading.

Have a look at yourselves and your church against this standard – God's standard of love and respect for one another.

Things to discuss

1 The people of Israel believed that Elijah would return to herald the coming of the Messiah. In what ways is John the Baptist similar to Elijah?

2 What makes us repentant? Why doesn't repentance lead to despair?

Justice and mercy

Thought for the day

If you are a sinner, then Jesus considers you a friend.

Things to read

Psalms 56, 57
Jeremiah 30:1-3, 10-22
Luke 13:1-17

Things to do

Aim: To explore the blend of righteousness and mercy in God's nature.

First read the passage from Jeremiah and pick out from it both justice and mercy. Now read the passage from Luke and identify the same qualities in Jesus during this situation. Give out some newspaper stories for people to discuss in twos or threes, and try to discover what happens when there is an imbalance or a misunderstanding of these qualities. How can Jesus' behaviour (both here and in other parts of the gospels) help us to tread the right path in delicate and difficult situations?

   Stick the pictures and headlines onto a chart and have a time of intercession for those involved in the situations. Provide stationery so that if it would help to write letters of protest or encouragement you can do so straight away.

Things to discuss

1 To what extent should we be understanding, and when should we speak out against sin?

2 Why didn't Jesus just keep strictly within the expected rules?

God's rebuilding programme

Thought for the day

No matter how ruined or damaged our lives are, God has plans for a full restoration programme and is ready to start work right away.

Things to read

Psalms 121, 126
Ezra 3
Revelation 3:1-13

Things to do

Aim: To look at rebuilding costs for individuals, and for the churches.

Start by reading Ezra 3, and then study the passage to discover:

1 which bit they rebuilt first
2 how they paid for the rebuilding materials
3 what the people were frightened of
4 how old the supervisors were
5 what happened when the foundations were laid
6 why some of the older people were weeping.

You could either do this as one group or in smaller groups of two or three.

Now read the passage from Revelation 3 and talk together about what makes for strong churches, and what kind of things make them weakened.

What things do these words to the churches in Sardis and Philadelphia alert us to which we need to address in our own churches and in ourselves?

Things to discuss

1 Notice that some of those who remembered the previous temple building were not grumbling and critical of the new model, but weeping. What does that suggest about their spiritual state of health?

2 How seriously do we take the priority of prayerful preparation in our own projects, our church events, and our country's policies and legislation? Make a note of any positive recommendations so that your discussion is fruitful.

Consequences

Thought for the day

In Jesus we are not just patched up but made new.

Things to read

Psalm 77
2 Samuel 12:1-18a
Acts 9:1-22

Things to do

Aim: To help them know about the dangers and consequences of sin, but above all of God's total forgiveness.

Read together the whole series of events which led to Uriah's killing, and Nathan's story. At this point, stop to discuss David's situation, the way things had gone from bad to worse, and why he had given in to temptation in the first place. (Was it something to do with staying behind instead of going out with his army? Or was he used to getting his own way as king? etc.)

Now go on to read the next section, looking at David's violent reaction to the man in the story and his subsequent confession and forgiveness. What does David's attitude to the baby suggest about his relationship with Bathsheba? In what way does God manage to retrieve every scrap of goodness in the situation and use it?

Explore some of these issues in a role play, having each character in order giving their version of the story and how they felt about it.

Characters: David, Uriah, Bathsheba, Nathan and one of the courtiers.

De-role the actors (see Foreword) and consider what all this can teach us about dealing with temptation and sin in our own lives.

Things to discuss

1 David understood that there would be consequences of his sin, although he had been forgiven. How does God show his mercy even here?

2 What can we learn in Acts 9 of the urgency of being constantly attentive to God?

Forgiving and being forgiven

Thought for the day

There's no better feeling than being restored to the God who loves you and to whom you belong.

Things to read

Psalms 85, 133
Deuteronomy 30:1-10
Matthew 18:10-22

Things to do

Aim: For them to understand Jesus' teaching on forgiveness.

Start by reading Deuteronomy, and then go straight on to the Matthew passage, noticing how in the real world we don't seem to have God's law in our hearts fully, so there is a desperate need to know what to do when we are sinned against. Jesus' teaching on forgiveness is backed up by his previous story of the lost sheep, and goes for sensitivity, understanding and compassion rather than condemnation. For all of us, this is easier said than done.

Talk together about the difficulties we have in forgiving, and look at some of the world's current problems to see if sinning against and/or lack of forgiveness are the cause. They nearly always are.

Using Jesus' parable and his direct teaching, sort out some practical ways in which we could work at our reactions to being insulted, ignored, gossiped about or otherwise sinned against.

Things to discuss

1 Are we able to forgive others better than we are able to forgive ourselves?

2 Do we put into practice Jesus' guidelines for dealing with people who sin against us – both as individuals and within our church community? Have we any systematic strategy or do we fight shy of tackling the problems through embarrassment? Is there any way we could improve matters?

Sin old and new

Thought for the day

We need to build up our defences against temptation.

Things to read

Psalm 119:9-24
1 Samuel 26
Luke 22:1-23

Things to do

Aim: To look at the similarities and differences between the Old Testament and New Testament passages, so as to explore the nature of temptation and sin.

Have a chart drawn up like this:

DIFFERENCES		SIMILARITIES	
1 Sam 26	Luke 22	1 Sam 26	Luke 22

Read the passages from 1 Samuel and Luke, either together or in two different groups and then work through them, writing in all that is similar and all that is different in them. Discuss what enables people to resist temptation in their lives, bringing out how important our relationship with God is in dealing effectively with temptation.

Things to discuss

1 How does the night visit in 1 Samuel affect the spiritual growth of a) Saul and b) David?

2 Where does temptation turn into sin and how can we stop that happening?

Valuing our birthright

Thought for the day   Sin destroys us: God can save us.

Things to read   Psalm 25
Isaiah 44:6-22
1 Corinthians 10:1-13 (or 24)

Things to do   *Aim:* To remind them of their true birthright.

Prepare a short tape – audio or video – of a selection of adverts on TV. Look at the ways they are persuading us to buy their product.

e.g. You will look beautiful if . . .
    You will be successful if . . .
    You will be acceptable if . . .

Talk together about some of the pressures they find themselves under to do what they know is wrong. Recognise the real difficulties here and offer sympathy, support and practical encouragement, not implied criticism or judgement.
Stress that God loves them and holds them very precious. That's why he has something far more lovely and fulfilling in store for them in their lives. Also, he completely understands all their temptations. If they stay close to God, he will protect them from being cheated out of the fulfilling life he has planned for them.

Things to discuss   1 What is the difference between enjoyment and idolatry?

2 What practical steps can we take to deal with temptation?

WORSHIP, DISCIPLESHIP, MISSION

Baptism: John and Jesus

Thought for the day   God gives us the grace necessary to reveal his glory.

Things to read   Psalms 46, 47
Genesis 8:15-9:17
Acts 18:24-19:6

Things to do   *Aim:* To look at the difference between John's baptism and baptism in the name of Jesus.

First read the Noah passage at the end of the flood, and the rainbow's promise. Talk together about the way the water both destroyed evil and gave new life.

Then go on to read the passage from Acts, pausing at the point where Apollos says he has only known John's baptism. See if the group can work out the difference between this baptism and the sort Paul is talking about. When you have had a go at this, read on to find out what answer the Bible gives. Make the connection between the sign of water and drowning here, and in the Noah story.

Look at the baptismal promises and suggest ways that the church can ensure that people really know what they are taking on when they come to be baptised. Take note of any suggestions and put them before the church, or church council meeting.

Things to discuss   1   As Priscilla and Aquila listened to Apollos, their visiting preacher, what do you think went through their minds? How can we learn from their way of dealing with the situation and Apollos' response?

2   Talk through the significance of the symbols of water and breath in the sacrament of baptism.

Legalism, law and grace

Thought for the day   God reveals himself through signs and wonders

Things to read   Psalms 135, 136
Nehemiah 13:15-22
John 5:1-21

Things to do   *Aim:* To see how God's glory was revealed in his fulfilling of the Law.

First read the Old Testament passage and explain its historical context for the people of Israel. (This was after their exile, when they were trying to make a fresh start and were determined to keep themselves as a race set apart from the surrounding nations. Sabbath keeping and no mixed marriages were the clear signs of this.) See if they can also sense any spiritual dangers in having such exact rules.

Now read the New Testament passage, either miming it or with different people reading different parts, and explore the link between the Jewish rule system and the teachers' attitude to Jesus' healing on the Sabbath. Why didn't Jesus keep to the rules if he was supposed to be fulfilling the Law? How in fact was this truly a fulfilling of the law? Are there any ways in which we prevent God's glory from radiating out because of complex rule systems which obscure the real truth?

Things to discuss   1 To what extent were the Jewish authorities right in what they said to the healed man, and to what extent were they tragically wrong?

2 It is always difficult to get the balance right between becoming self-righteous on the one hand and self-indulgent on the other. How can we address this in our lives and in evangelism?

The spirit of the law

Thought for the day

God reveals his glory in the way he rebuilds and restores.

Things to read

Psalm 34
1 Samuel 21:1-6
Matthew 12:1-21

Things to do

Aim: For them to look at what the law of God really means.

Start by reading together the passage from 1 Samuel 21. What do they think about what happened here? Was it right for David and his army to eat the sacred bread?

Now read the passage from Matthew 12 and then have small groups working on role plays where two are Pharisees and two are disciples discussing Jesus' behaviour.

De-role the actors (see Foreword) and share the discoveries of the groups. Are there any rules in our own church which might sometimes get in the way of the real truth, instead of making it clearer? Take note of what is said and act on it by praying together for guidance as to what should be done.

Things to discuss

1 What do you think you would have done in Ahimelech's situation? He and his family paid a terrible price for helping David (1 Samuel 22).

2 There is often conflict in Christian families when Sunday activities clash with church times and so on. Having read Jesus' teaching about the Sabbath, how do you think we should organise our weekends?

Prayer first, action second

Thought for the day

God not only shows us the route, but walks with us each step of the way.

Things to read

Psalms 57, 63:1-9
Nehemiah 1
1 Corinthians 15:1-28

Things to do

Aim: To put into practice the head knowledge of prayer first, action second.

First ask them to put in order a list of stages for washing an elephant, or making a honey and Marmite sandwich. (My daughter actually chooses to make and eat these!) Or you could write the stages beforehand and let them sort them.

Read the passage from Nehemiah, explaining enough background for them to understand his reason for panic. Then look at the order of his actions, noting that prayer comes first.

Next look at Paul's letter to the Church in Corinth. Try to think what might have been going on that caused Paul to write all this. He must have already been through the horror and sadness stage, and the praying, so that this letter was his resulting action.

Show them some issues which cause us distress. Together pray openly and expectantly, and then put into practice the plan of action that seems right. Bear in mind that the ideas may not come in your short session; ask everyone to continue praying and discuss ideas next time. It may well be that other events will happen which link up and lead you forward in a particular way.

Things to discuss

1 Work through Nehemiah's prayer to see the pattern and content, and learn from it some good ideas about how to pray.

2 If we really believe that there is life after death, and that heaven will be an endless time of joy and beauty in God's presence, what difference will that make to the way we live our lives?

God's love is for all

Thought for the day

God's saving news of love is not for a few, but for every person in every nation.

Things to read

Psalm 119:41-56
Jonah 3 and 4
Acts 13:1-13

Things to do

Aim: To look at some of God's surprising choices.

Begin with a game of choice such as Pairs or Pontoon, so that they are made aware of the way we are always making choices, and these are often 'blind' choices where we don't have enough information to do much more than guess. Introduce the Jonah story, filling in the first part, before reading together chapters 3 and 4.

Discuss why Jonah felt so angry, and how God helped him understand. Then look at the first part of the Acts reading, where Paul and Barnabas were chosen. If they had chosen without fasting and prayer it would have been a blind choice, because they had no way of knowing what kind of situations these two would meet on the new mission. Asking God was, in a way, like being able to use inside information and so get the best people for the job.

If we ask him, God will always help us like this.

Things to discuss

1 Why did Jonah get so angry? Do you see his point? Do you think he was justified?

2 As we can see from this passage from Acts, the spread of the gospel is bound to lead us into contact with evil and we need to be prepared. Look at how Paul and Barnabas and the Church prepared, and draw up a possible preparation plan for use in your own area.

Loving as God loves us

Thought for the day   We are to love others in the way God loves us – completely.

Things to read   Psalm 81
Deuteronomy 24:10-end
1 John 3:13-end

Things to do   *Aim:* To help them see how love can be translated into practical caring.

Read the Deuteronomy passage, explaining how compassionate and caring these laws were in comparison to the other ancient laws of neighbouring cultures. Then look at the John reading, to see what he considers real loving to involve. Look at the expense of love, and the necessity of acting it out, rather than just waffling on about it.
    Either in small groups or all together, work out a composite 'recipe' for living God's loving way, which can then be published in the magazine or on next week's handout.
    Here is one recipe to give you the idea.

1 Take one family aching with hunger, home destroyed, eyes full of fear.
2 Gather some consciences from well-fed Christians and prick them thoroughly.
3 When hearts have softened wait for action to start.
4 Fill needs to the brim and hold carefully, to avoid smashing hopes and lives.

Things to discuss   1 Are there any laws/acceptable behaviour in our society which exploit the vulnerable and the poor? What would be a more Godly way of doing things?

2 It has been said that our wallet is the last part of us to get converted. How far do you think this is true?

Practical evangelism

Thought for the day

It is both our privilege and our responsibility to spread the good news wherever we are put.

Things to read

Psalms 145, 150
Amos 5:14-24 (or 6-24)
Romans 15:14-29

Things to do

Aim: To explore the practicalities of spreading the faith.

Begin by looking at a selection of estate-agency brochures for houses in the area. In groups of two or three, choose a favourite for a family/a bachelor/an elderly couple. Share the results of the discussions.

Point out that unless the news of those properties had been made available, the potential buyers would never have known about them; very few would go to the trouble of driving round every street and knocking on doors, asking whether the house was for sale. Yet sometimes we keep the good news of our faith shut tight in our churches where no one hears of it. How can we make sure that people know about Jesus in a way which they understand and which doesn't frighten them off?

Have a brainstorming session for plans of how the church can witness to different groups of people, and have the resulting list of ideas presented to the next church or council meeting. Finish with Paul's letter to the Romans, hearing his plans for the spread of the Early Church, and pray together for the people in the area who have yet to be introduced to Jesus.

Things to discuss

1 Time and again it is hypocrisy which galls the heart of God. Why do you think this is so? Is there anything that smacks of hypocrisy or double standards which needs addressing among Christians today?

2 It almost makes us tired just reading about Paul's enthusiastic travel plans in order to win Gentiles for God. Are we as passionate for the spread of the gospel? Why/why not?

Christianity, authority and protest

Thought for the day

God's power enables us to be more fully ourselves.

Things to read

Psalm 50
1 Samuel 8:4-22a
1 Peter 2:11-end

Things to do

Aim: To explore our attitude to authority as Christians.

Begin by reading the passage from 1 Samuel. Talk together about why the people wanted a king, and why Samuel wasn't so keen. Remember that they were surrounded by pagan societies. Now read the passage from 1 Peter, so that they can see Peter's advice as to the way we should behave. At that time the Christians were living in a strongly pagan society, and facing increasing persecution for their faith.

What about in our own time, when it is supposedly accepted that people shouldn't put up with bad treatment but protest loudly until things are changed? Do they think this is actually true? Are there some categories of people in our society who do not or cannot complain (such as the mentally vulnerable, the homeless or, in some countries, women and children or those of a low caste)? Keep track of the discussion by jotting down main points and suggest that they finish the session by expressing some of their feelings in paint or creative writing. Let the sharing lead on to a time of prayer, proclaiming the Lordship of Jesus in all the sadness, neglect and corruption of the world.

Things to discuss

1 Why did the people want a king? What were Samuel's objections?

2 Why does Peter insist upon us putting up with authority, even if it treats us badly? At what point do we fight against evil, and what form should such a battle take?

A dangerous faith

Thought for the day
Commit your ways to God; he promises to look after your needs and he will not let you down.

Things to read
Psalm 37:1-22
Joshua 23
2 Corinthians 11:16-31

Things to do
Aim: For them to see how dangerous/exciting the Christian life can be when we live it fully.

Start by reading the passage from Corinthians and then showing a section from *The cross and the switchblade*, so that they can see that the dangers were not just there during Paul's life. It still gets dangerous today when people speak out for what is right and experience hostility.

If you have never experienced one of the Christian adventure holidays for young people, this might be a good time to introduce the idea. Such experiences are especially valuable if you are small in numbers. Or suggest the possibility of planning a hike with other churches in the area, praying your way through the town or getting involved with a local evangelism project.

Pray together about where God is leading you as a group, and be prepared for ideas which may surprise or even disappoint you.

Things to discuss
1 Much of what Joshua says is to do with being in the world but not of it. How does that apply to us today?

2 Paul's life was exceptionally dangerous, but, even so, does it challenge our expectations of living quietly and comfortably as Christians?

Do as you would be done by

Thought for the day

Treat others as you would like them to treat you.

Things to read

Psalm 107:1-32
1 Kings 21
Matthew 7:1-12

Things to do

Aim: To explore the Naboth story and how Jesus taught us to treat one another.

First read the Naboth story in small groups with different people taking the different parts, and then in the full group have a role play with Ahab, Jezebel, Naboth and the hired men giving their accounts of the events. Then de-role the actors (see Forword).

On a large sheet of paper, draw some steps going down, and try to work out together what stages Ahab and Jezebel might have gone through to reach this point of total selfishness without concern for others. It may alert us to the dangers of the early steps in our own lives.

Now look at the passage from Matthew 7. Do our laws reflect these teachings? Does our behaviour, as a country, a church and as individuals? If you find any glaring inconsistencies, draft letters or plan other action which seems appropriate to bring about a change for the better.

Things to discuss

1 Have a go at tracing the possible steps and behaviour patterns which eventually led to this act by Ahab and Jezebel.

2 Work through the advice Jesus gives about the way we treat one another, trying to keep open minded and attentive to what God may be saying to you, the church, or the community in which you live. Each section seems obvious at first sight, through familiarity, but be ready to be challenged.

In God's likeness

Thought for the day

Since we are made in God's likeness, the only real and fulfilling way to live is in a loving, Godlike way.

Things to read

Psalm 81
Genesis 50:15-end
1 John 2:1-17

Things to do

Aim: To look at living as a Christian in the real world.

Begin with a ball team game appropriate to the surroundings, and talk over the need to make quick, good decisions so as to enable the whole team to do well. In life, we are always having to make decisions about the way we act, and some of those choices we make have lasting effects and can change or threaten to ruin our lives. Read the Genesis passage, and discuss how Joseph's brothers might have felt. What good had God managed to bring out of their wrong behaviour?

Read the John passage and lead them to see the importance of acting on what we believe, rather than just talking about it. Have a selection of leaflets about organisations which need support (either financial, practical or prayer support) and decide together on something that you could take on as individuals or in groups to put your faith into action.

Things to discuss

1 What does Joseph's reply to his brothers show us about his character and his relationship with God?

2 There is always the need to tread the fine line between fully accepting God's forgiveness and living life to the full on one hand, and presuming on God's forgiveness and living carelessly on the other. How do Joseph and John help us to tackle this issue?

Jesus and prayer

Thought for the day

God is far more ready to lavish his blessings on us than we are to receive them.

Things to read

Psalms 65, 67
Deuteronomy 28:1-14
Luke 10:38-11:13

Things to do

Aim: For them to learn more about the different aspects of prayer as expressed in the Lord's Prayer – praise and thanksgiving, intercession and petition, penitence and commitment.

First read together Psalm 65 and then the reading from Luke. Consider some of these points:

Is Jesus praising Mary for being lazy?
What does 'listening' mean if we can't hear Jesus answering us?
In what ways does Jesus speak to us?
What is the Lord's Prayer teaching us about praying?

Go through the Lord's Prayer section by section so that it challenges our present level of prayer and encourages us to pray with more confidence. Suggest that they keep a prayer diary and check it often to see for themselves how God does indeed answer prayer. This session may open up some disappointments, doubts and misunderstandings. Deal honestly and lovingly with each point so that young people who are learning to explore and question their faith can do so in an atmosphere of safety and mutual respect.

Things to discuss

1 In what ways does corruption in our society make for misery and fear in people's lives?

2 How can we learn to ask for what is in harmony with God's will?

The meaning of authority

Thought for the day

Prophets say what we need to hear – not what we want to hear.

Things to read

Psalms 57, 63:1-9
Numbers 22:36-23:12
Luke 16:19-end

Things to do

Aim: To explore the nature of God's authority compared with ours.

Bring a few national newspapers and give them out to small groups, asking everyone to pick out stories which show someone acting in authority. Give each group a chart with two columns. In one column they name the person acting in authority, and in the other comment on their decision or action, such as 'wise', 'foolish', 'thoughtless' or 'evil'.

Join into one group to share the findings. They will no doubt have found a considerable number of instances which highlight human weakness and make us thankful that we are not ultimately in charge of creation.

Now read the Dives story, and talk about the way Dives still half expected to organise God and then bargain with him, even after death. There may be an alarming amount of evil in this world, but through dying and being raised from death, Jesus' love has won the final victory over all that is thoughtless, unwise, destructive, cruel and hopeless.

Things to discuss

1 What similarities can you find between Balak and Dives?

2 Are we prepared to let God do the organising and planning with us in our lives/church?

Compassionate prayer

Thought for the day   'I bring life.'

Things to read
Psalm 49:1-6
Exodus 32:1-14
Luke 7:11-17

Things to do

Aim: To raise awareness of the need to feel compassion as we plead for our world.

Read the passage from Luke together, and talk about Jesus' compassion for the widow which made him respond in action.

Focus today on a particular need. There may be something which the church is particularly involved with; there may be an area which God leads you to look at as you prepare the session. Whatever it is – drug abuse, homelessness, famine, local unemployment, families in stress – come prepared with information, pictures, articles, case studies and so on. Have a time of sharing all the material around, and perhaps invite someone personally involved to talk informally and discuss the problem.

The aim is to take the problem out of the general into the particular, so that we can pray with love and sympathy, standing alongside those who suffer.

Things to discuss

1 Why did the people of Israel go astray so quickly? What can we learn about our outreach programme – do we provide sufficient nurture for people when they first join the community?

2 What do we learn about the character of God from Jesus' behaviour in the passage from Luke?

Conflicts and dangers

Thought for the day

Following Christ is not always a comfortable place to be.

Things to read

Psalm 119:73-88
Genesis 37:1-28
Luke 22:24-53 (or 39-53)

Things to do

Aim: To look at some of the conflicts and dangers which Christians face.

You will need a selection of books and information about Christians who risk extreme hardship, persecution or other danger for practising their Christian faith. Some examples are: Brother Damian, Martin Luther King, William Wilberforce, Sister Emanuel, Desmond Tutu, Terry Waite, Mother Teresa, St Clare, Florence Nightingale, and any local unsung heroes and heroines in your church.

Read the passage from Luke together, noticing how Jesus prays so deeply for the agony to be avoided but recognises that he must go through with it.

Consider the areas in our own lives where being a Christian makes for unavoidable conflict, and encourage one another by praying for these difficult situations and all the people involved.

Things to discuss

1 Judas betrayed Jesus with a gesture of friendship, which must have been particularly hurtful. Does the church (or do we as individual Christians) sometimes betray Jesus under cover of being his friends?

2 Families are often full of feuds and jealousies. Is there any way to avoid this, or do we just have to accept it?

Growing pains

Thought for the day	God reveals his glory in the way he rebuilds and restores.

Things to read

Psalm 34
Zechariah 8:1-7
Acts 15:1-21

Things to do

Aim: To look at how the Early Church coped with a difficult problem in the process of God's development programme.

Split the group into two and have both groups working on the passage in Acts. In each case they need to read it together, one group sympathising with the Jewish viewpoint, the other as Gentiles. Then come together to have a short role discussion which identifies the problem and helps them see how feelings ran high.

De-role the members (see Foreword) and work through the passage together, noting the order of events so as to see how the problem was tackled and resolved. (The willingness to listen to one another, to change where necessary, to pray together – all these are very noticeable.) Beside the events, work out a possible model we could use in contemporary disputes in the Church and pray expectantly about this.

Things to discuss

1 Imagine yourself into the position of these people of Israel, in exile from their own country. Think how Zechariah's words might have affected you.

2 Work through the different stages of the Jew/Gentile problem of the Early Church. What can we learn from the way the problem was tackled and resolved?

Everyone included

Thought for the day God's salvation is for all peoples and nations; everyone is eligible.

Things to read Psalm 89:19-38
Isaiah 43:1-13
Matthew 1

Things to do *Aim:* To reflect on the value of families, and look at Jesus' family.

Read the Matthew passage together, linking the events with the current tragedy of refugees having to leave their countries to avoid danger. Notice the kind of character Joseph was, and talk about why God had chosen him to help bring up his Son.

Now show some pictures with different images of 'family' and talk about what they think of as an ideal family; which qualities they associate with a good father, or a good mother. In the discussion refer to the family God chose for Jesus, and don't let it degenerate into a moans session. Be open and sensitive to any real problems which are raised and bring these into a time of prayer for our own and all family life, which is so often difficult as well as beneficial. Remind everyone that we are also part of the wider family of God, who loves us like the very best parent, only more so.

Things to discuss 1 There are still so many who do not realise that God is *their* God and loves them. What are we/should we be doing about this?

2 Look up the Micah prophecy which the scribes at Herod's palace found. What prevented it from being good news for Herod? What kind of things can block our receptivity and obedience to God?

God's word, old and new

Thought for the day

The word of God has been gradually unfolded all through the Old Testament, throughout the New Testament and ever since.

Things to read

Psalm 119:137-152
1 Kings 22:1-28
Romans 10:5-17

Things to do

Aim: To help them see the importance of having God's word in our hearts.

First read the Romans passage together. Talk about the differences between following rules and believing with your heart, and how these affect your actions in different ways. Give as examples such things as 'Don't spread gossip'; 'Drive or cycle on the left'; 'Keep your body for the person you marry'.

It may well be that one thing which crops up is that we often know what's right but still want to carry on in our own way.

Now read 1 Kings 22:1-17, with different people taking speaking parts. Discuss this reading in the light of what was said earlier – look at the stages and consequences of Ahab's behaviour. Then pray together for God's word to take root in our hearts and change us from the inside.

Things to discuss

1 Whom do we go to when we want to talk things over or get advice – people who know the Lord well, or people who are likely to agree with us? What are the advantages/ disadvantages of both?

2 It's tempting to speak the truth only when it won't get us into difficult or embarrassing situations. But what does this suggest about who really is the Lord of our hearts and minds?

INDEX OF USES

INDEX OF BIBLICAL CHARACTERS

Jesus is not included in this index since the category would contain so high a proportion of the book as to be of little practical use.

INDEX OF BIBLICAL REFERENCES